SCHOLASTIC
News
Nonfiction Readers

George Washington Carver

by
Jo S. Kittinger

Children's Press®
A Division of Scholastic Inc.
New York Toronto London Auckland Sydney
Mexico City New Delhi Hong Kong
Danbury, Connecticut

These content vocabulary builders
are for grades 1-2.

Consultant: David Ernesto Romero
President, Sigma Lambda Beta, Omicron Chapter
Iowa State University

Curriculum Specialist: Linda Bullock

Photo Credits:

Photographs © 2005: AP/Wide World Photos: cover; Corbis Images/Lance Nelson: 5 top left, 10; Culver Pictures: 4 bottom right, 8; Envision Stock Photography Inc./Steven Mark Needham: 23 bottom left, 23 top left; Getty Images/Hulton Archive: 5 bottom left, 7; New York Public Library, Schomburg Center for Research in Black Culture: 17; Peter Arnold Inc./Walter H. Hodge: 4 bottom left, 12, 13; Photri Inc./A. Gibson: 5 top right, 19; PictureQuest/BananaStock: 23 bottom right; Superstock, Inc.: 23 top right (Michael Rutherford), 2, 15; Tuskegee University Archives: 5 bottom right, 11 (George Washington Carver National Monument), back cover (P. H. Polk/Iowa State University Library, Special Collections); USDA: 1, 4 top, 9.

Book Design: Simonsays Design!

Library of Congress Cataloging-in-Publication Data

Kittinger, Jo S.
  George Washington Carver / by Jo S. Kittinger.
     p. cm. – (Scholastic news nonfiction readers)
  Includes bibliographical references (p.   ) and index.
  ISBN 0-516-24939-8 (lib. bdg.)   0-516-24782-4 (pbk.)
  1. Carver, George Washington, 1864?-1943–Juvenile literature.
  2. African American agriculturists–Biography–Juvenile literature.
  3. Agriculturists–United States–Biography–Juvenile literature. I. Title.
  II. Series.
  S417.C3K58 2005
  630'.92–dc22
                                                      2005002103

19 20 21 22 23 R 19 18 17

CONTENTS

WORD HUNT

Look for these words as you read. They will be in **bold**.

cotton
(**kot**-uhn)

peanut
(**pee**-nuht)

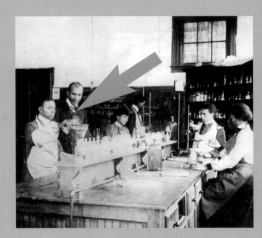

scientist
(**sye**-uhn-tist)

George W. Carver
(jorj **kar**-ver)

museum
(myoo-**zee**-um)

slaves
(slayvs)

soil
(soyl)

Meet George Washington Carver

Can you imagine being a **slave**?

A slave is a person owned by another person.

George Washington Carver was born a slave in Missouri around 1864.

Soon after he was born, all slaves were set free.

These are slaves working in a field.

George worked hard so he could go to school.

He went to college in Iowa.

George became a teacher and a **scientist**.

scientist

George

George wanted to help poor farmers.

Their **soil** was bad from planting **cotton** every year.

But what else could the farmers plant?

cotton

soil

George knew that planting the same thing every year was bad for soil.

The farmers could plant **peanuts**!

Peanuts would help the soil.

But farmers did not think they could sell peanuts.

peanut

Peanuts grow under the soil.

So, George invented 300 things people could make with peanuts.

He made paper, soap, and paint from peanuts.

He made peanut milk.

He made candy, too.

George also used peanuts to make food for animals.

Now the farmers knew
they could sell peanuts.

George and his helper
Austin kept inventing
new ways to use peanuts.

George Washington Carver and Austin W. Curtis work in the lab.

George became famous.

But he never cared about money.

He only wanted to help people.

George died in 1943. There is a **museum** named after him.

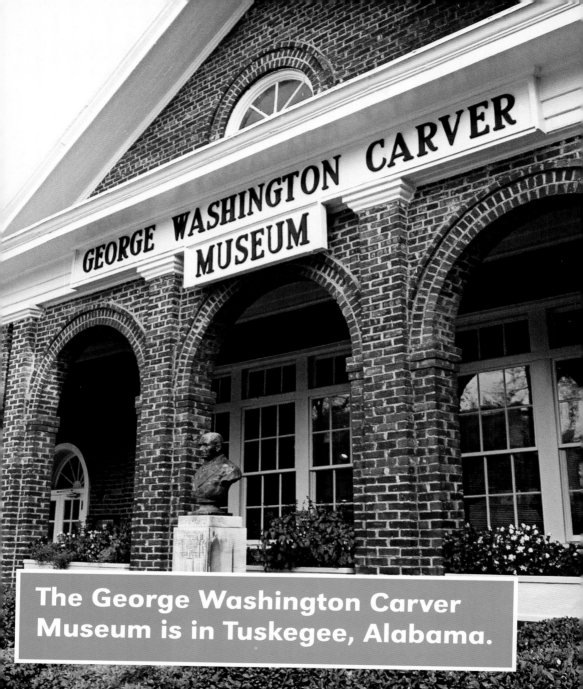

The George Washington Carver Museum is in Tuskegee, Alabama.

HOW DO PEANUTS

1

A peanut
is planted.

2

In 10 days, the
plant sprouts.

3

The plant
grows larger.

GROW?

In 35 days, the plant blooms.

In 50 days, pegs enter the soil.

In 60 days, the pegs swell. They turn into peanuts.

YOUR NEW WORDS

George W. Carver (jorj **kar**-ver)
a scientist who invented 300 things
from peanuts

cotton (**kot**-uhn) a plant that grows balls
of soft white fibers

museum (myoo-**zee**-um) a place where
interesting objects are kept

peanut (**pee**-nuht) a seed that looks like
a nut; it grows underground

scientist (**sye**-uhn-tist) a person who works
with science

slaves (slayvz) people owned by
other people

soil (soyl) dirt in which plants grow

FOUR THINGS MADE WITH PEANUTS

granola bar

peanut brittle

peanut butter

peanut oil

INDEX

FIND OUT MORE

Book:

George Washington Carver, by Rebecca Gomez, ABDO Publishing, 2003.

Website:

George Washington Carver Crafts and Activities
www.daniellesplace.com/html/georgecarver.html

MEET THE AUTHOR:

Jo S. Kittinger enjoys nature and science, like George W. Carver. She writes books for children about the things she loves. She lives in Hoover, Alabama.